Ordinary Monsters

MONGREL EMPIRE PRESS
NORMAN, OKLAHOMA, UNITED STATES OF AMERICA

2017

FIRST EDITION, 2017

Ordinary Monsters
© 2017 by Justin Bond

ISBN 978-0-9972517-8-4

Cover Art & Design
© 2017 by Holly Samson Hall

Author Photo

Mongrel Empire Press
Norman, OK

Online catalogue: www.mongrelempire.org

This publisher is a proud member of

COUNCIL OF LITERARY MAGAZINES & PRESSES
w w w . c l m p . o r g

Ordinary Monsters

Justin Bond

Contents

The Postulant

Circes, thy monsters painted out the hue
of feigned filthiness, but ours is true.

Thomas Bastard
Book 7, Epigram 42

And as you lie in bed
like an effigy of yourself,
it is the ordinary that comes to save you—

Linda Pastan
The Ordinary

The Lover

Handsome Young Man

The light moves in other directions,
the way he appears to watch
and look up at one time.
Know your role: hold the spoon
and make yourself useful.
Know your center: we inherit
the grave, but for the sake of joy
we keep our eyes set away from it.

Something reminded me of what I wanted to tell you

It was the trash collecting in the fence along the expressway, looking almost like a roadside memorial to a terrible accident or a dead princess, which can sometimes be the same thing. But you are not a fence, though some days we are two cars turning in opposite directions at the same stop, and I fight the urge to jerk the wheel and accelerate into the smooth expanse of your gleaming side just to remind you I am capable of it.

The Weight of Longing

Imagine a body like a board,
slight and rough-hewn.

Who's that trip-trapping over my bridge?

In a room we once consulted the maps
of our bodies in dark corners.

Palms dimpled from the rivets in a boy's jeans.
The sport in choosing the next bruise.

How many little deaths have I suffered
to name this anything other than love?

The weight of it, the debt of this longing.
How I splinter even as I burn.

Stiff Upper Lip

When I cradle the softest part of you in my palm,
in the rolling weight I feel the stirring of verbs restless for conjugation.

Will leave. Is leaving. Has left.

Already it is May, and from the bridge the skyline
lists like crooked teeth in the loose jaw of the river.

Already the days bend over and into themselves,
dog-eared pages of a book I've read & reread.

O barn swallow, o low-slung eaves! Red whip of wind.
The clutch of featherless bodies flung like fistfuls of apricots

in the surf of the summer's surge, the weathered boards
that give like a body loved to the point of breaking.

So much of me has been made a mountain,
but I have never aspired to more than these sloping hills

and valleys of pencil shavings, these rivers of sap.

The Right Way to Want Me

The
way
Madonna
wants
to
devour
Lady Gaga
probably
head
first
strand
by
strand
of
bleached
blonde
ambition
the
super
ego
subsuming
the
id
unless
you
would
consider
that
reductive

Desiderata

In the valley the treetops
are bandaged in a dirty gauze
the fields lusty with flames set
to start another growing season
from the tired earth

I could clothe myself in birdcalls
the meadowlark, the scissortail

What is left to do
when the skeletons have left the closets

When they rattle around the house
like robots of blown glass
pulling up the carpets
and rearranging furniture

To leave
or burn it down

Sometimes I worry
that I will never yield
enough to sustain you
that like a fallow field
I have given the best of myself
to past seasons

I read a story once of a Russian saint
who when gifted doves by her enemies

tied lit kindling to their feet
and sent them home to flutter ruin
down upon what she could not possess

Imagine how lovely they must have seemed
drifting like rogue stars from the night sky

in the way that all gone things
shine brightest in the moment
of their losing

Searchlights

1.

In the mirror I trace the red rash
the cat left on my cheek.
For an hour, maybe two, after you leave
I watch the ugly braille raise up and darken.
Deep enough I worry it will linger
until morning, long enough
that I can't be sure you're coming back.
Time passes like water running down
a yawning throat of sink.
Boards creak beneath
the neighbor's bare feet.
Even the floor is worn out with her.

2.

The story of us
is the story of America:
brief, tumultuous. Mostly true.
A series of false starts
we like to call resilience.
Sartre said Freedom is what you do
with what's been done to you,
so we pave over the wagon wheel
ruts of our pasts and spend money
buying stuff to fill the empty parking lot
we live in, because we know not everyone
is cut out for making it on their own.
At the end of it, we meant well.

3.

What is love, if not addiction?
Desire distilled down
to one distinct and desperate purpose of thought.
Knowing that even if you returned to me damaged, somehow less
than I hoped you would be, reeking of regret
and the river and the men who linger there,

I would baptize you in a swirling surge of forgiveness,
dark and unrelenting as the water spilling
over the lip of the low-water dam
where only hours ago searchlights lit the shore
like a carnival, a body on the bank
and three more still missing.

4.
I don't believe the river
revels in her squalor.
That she intended anything other than love
when she wombed them like a mother
too lonely to let them go.

Bare trees and fallen branches, everywhere

Winter only hangs on long enough for us to forget the winters that came before.
It's time slowed to stasis, the mess of the world tucked away in deep pockets
that hedges us in quiet rumination the way a snow drift can debilitate the city.
Roads rendered impassable, cars and trucks abandoned, the silence so profound
you begin to wonder if the rest of the world has been raptured without you.
It's easy to live in the past when everything is a rerun,
when we spend half our time checking the mirrors to see what is behind us.
Dogs have no sense of history, any scattering squirrel could be the last or the next.
With the opening of a door every anxious minute alone evaporates like a bad dream.
We have so much to learn about joy, about the art of forgetfulness.
Last summer we discovered an orchid blooming behind the compost heap.
My memories of you spring up sudden and unexpected, never where they ought to be.
Your ghost always wears the same clothes, it forever rattles the same chains.
It treads the rug threadbare, waiting like a dog for me to come home and remember you.

You Don't Ask An Insect to Read Entomology

Night creeps in on cagey footfalls. I watch the men
trudge up from the riverbank two at a time,
wearing the stink of the water like a ripe agenda.
You are somewhere eating dinner with people I don't know.
Plates of chicken wings and cheese fries,
tiny hamburgers no bigger than a biscuit, and I am starving.
What a stew I could make from the leavings of strangers,
potatoes and leeks, my open, beautiful face.

Ad Infinitum

Towards the end
of a nervous breakdown,
I find myself
speaking in tongues.

I don't know
that I can ever see you.

A single drop of liquor
will send a scorpion
into a frenzy
of self destruction.

Oh, dead love,
I am speaking to you now.

Do This One Thing

Gather the bodies of the men.
I do not want to be haunted by them.

The chalk outlines hidden beneath the bed, my fingerprints everywhere.
The forgotten names scrawled in the margins of old books

yellowing alongside scratched-out arithmetic
and desiccated grocery lists.

The fact of death is a blade that whittles wood from the living.
They have been dead to me for years.

(They are not really dead)
((This is a kind of revenge))

I had a splintered dream of an ark of them, lashed together
with dirty sheets and sealed with pitch.

There was, of course, some struggling.
But in the end I had no need of God's cubits

I measured in knuckles and kneecaps,
a prow of bare sternums.

Left listing in the shallows, they saw me too late: there among the rocks,
a seal's skin lying next to me, washing my hair.

Waiting to frolic and glory in their brokenness.
In the shattered elbows, in the grimy backs of knees.

The blood & piss & shit & semen.
Who am I to deny all the body has to give?
You were with me, once.
A room in a house I did not know,

cool and damp as a cave by the sea.
Outside the window, the irises spread open,

trembled close enough to touch.
The moon came hard through the thin veil of cloud

that hung limp as the old sock
draped carelessly over the lampshade.

Partly in earnest, partly in jest

the spirits said, what has happened to us?
the old landmarks, the livery stable,
our horse and trap

but you were lost in science

they were suspicious of the present
the new bricks and mortar, strange atmospheres
behind doors that burned for haunting

but you were lost in science

the clock struck twelve and still the grave
could not quarter them

they strung the night like a bit, tugged the hairs
that wisped the corners of your rangy mouth

but you were lost in science

Mirth

In my dreams, it's always the tableau vivant, her arm
an arabesque of porcelain against the sheening damask.
The red hair burning like coiled copper wire

at the end of sleep's long dark hallway.
Down on Detroit the Greyhound station is teeming
with life, so many comings and goings,

as if the city were a room to be walked into or out of.
The fat woman with her stern face and trash bags full of secrets glowers
like a matriarch from her perch in the blank space between the streetlights.

I could measure beauty in half truths and still
never in my life feel this honest.
Thirty-one years and these hands are as idle

as an empty cigarette case, fingers that remember in stains:
a long and solitary train ride, the platform of lessons taught by the body.
The art of gathering flesh the way a milliner gathers yards of silk,

pinning and tucking the feathers and lace to recreate
the memory of a lady's hat on a hot summer afternoon.
A laugh on the breeze tinkling like the trees shaking

February from their branches.
The arteries of this city rupture and bleed asphalt.
A ruined mansion, unwilling to surrender its ghosts.

Troublesome Creek

Dance with the one what brung you. This man who seemed to me the Wild Man of Borneo, blue as the fog that drifted down the ridge at twilight, exotic as a feathered bed. Mama warned against false idols: the golden calf, the lure of Baal's legions.   But I ran hike-skirted and ululating, flossy and frangible as a laurel bush begging to be planted along the sandy swell of the creek bank.

Dance with the one what brung you. And if the first babies, come purple as bruised plums bursting between my thighs, were the sturm of thunderclaps ringing like shots through the hollow, the pink ones that came in time were no more than the drang of a house groaning as it settles.

Dance with the one what brung you. Even when they called us cursed, for what could be more blessed than the sweet murmur of the water swanning like silver over stone, the children drifting careless as haints amongst the frondling pines.

Movie Bachelors At Home, 1935

Say you were a broken boomerang and I had a mean left hook.
What fable would flood like a bruise, what monsters would spring
from the blood flung across a distance we could never recover?
Once you've borne witness to something beautiful and doomed—
Cary Grant and Randall Scott in a pool in Santa Monica,
sleek as otters, their naked shoulders not quite touching—
you begin to understand the stirring you feel every time you see
the handsome young widower down the hall, the one
with the puppy dog eyes and rough, unshaven jaw
who drags around the memory of his dead bride like a pieta.
It's as natural as sighing, as brushing up against him on the bus.
Misery is a greenhouse gas and we are polar ice caps, puddling.

The Night Ferry: A Love Poem

On the ferry Vincent stood behind me,
her hand resting against the small of my back.

The night reflected below us dark and deep
as a wood, whispering cantos against the hull of the ship.

Vincent said, There are no stars here:
only the light, and what the light cannot pass through.

She pressed a pear to my lips,
insistent as a mother, saying

Always at night, this falling into
of dark places, over and over.

My lips parted in spite of myself,
the flesh gritting like sleep between my gnashing teeth.

Seeing, keenly centered

You study the lamp, how its light
resolves his body in narrowing links.

The important thing was simply
the effort in rowing through another hard year.

The cautious hand taken,
the fear that dimmed beneath the elms,
all trivial in proportion.

Ocean Song

Waiting is its own invitation.
If I learn to yearn the way the sea
yearns, endlessly and without honor,
would you return to me?
The way some men spend their lives
diving into the wreck over and over
in their longing to return to the womb.

Afterthoughts

It's usually after the second drink
I allow my mind to wander
to thoughts of you and your new life.
I've heard the descriptions, of course.
Blonde and scruffy, shorter than me.
Probably younger.
The sex, I'm sure, is vigorous
and plentiful, unencumbered as it is
by bills and veterinary appointments,
arguments over money and the weight
that years can place on two bodies
with nothing left to discover.
I imagine you after, slick-backed
and breathless in a room
whose paint color I chose, and my heart
thrums like an iron lung.
It isn't jealousy I feel.
I have taken my love elsewhere,
life moves forward and I move with it.
It's the niggling worry of why
we didn't work, what part of the equation
I got wrong and if I might do it again.
It's knowing if I met you both
face to face, at the grocery or in a bar,
he would never see himself in me
the way I see myself in him.

How to Take A Long Walk in the Woods with the Person You Love

Lesson #1

It is important you never take your surroundings for granted.
The wild places of the world are called wild for a reason:
they do not wait for you to notice them.

You may be set upon by the blue lake.
The soft-spoken bobwhite, the fruitless grapevine unfurling
from the highest cottonwood branch to snake along the forest floor.

Beware the blunted tail.
Beware the leaves of three.
Beware the green sky.

The wild places of the world
are called wild for a reason: sometimes
the color of the sky will be your only warning.

Strange Fruit

Watching you browse the produce aisle at the supermarket is a study in
unbridled optimism. The consideration you devote to even the damaged
fruit: the soft melon, the withered plum. The way you run your thumb
along the ridges of an artichoke, as though you might give voice to a song
stifled in the green overlapping of a hundred mouthless tongues. At
home, I take an artichoke to bed and imagine it is your rough sex grazing
the damp doorways the hinges of my body would open and close for you,
a song in my ribs sharp as lemon rind.

You Will Remember This Differently

It is such a simple thing
the sunlight streaming, cold and clarion,
through the naked window.
The morning is young and you are snoring softly.
Soon you will wake and we will blue
these sheets like tobacco smoke,
because these are early days
and our bodies burn for touching,
but for the moment I am alone
with the stirring city, the broken staccato
of its kinetic heart: car horns blaring,
somewhere a siren, a woman laughing
over the din of a building going up
down the block,
as the light loses itself
in the luster of your dark curls
reminding me there is always
a little light to be found
even where it is too dark to see it.

The Wind Cuts Like Glass

The farther into the park we venture,
the fewer walkers we encounter.
It could be Vermont or Vladivostok;
the snow, the voracity of its sameness,
a reminder that whatever hold we claim
on this place is merely temporary.
We do not know the way
but do not say so,
we move with purpose
beneath the bending oak.
We do not name this:
the frosted face of the frozen lake,
the stream's stifled melody,
the feathered grace of the swallow
who dips in the shadow of the old stone bridge
to bless the snow that harbors there.

The Soldier

The Steam Cars on Monday

Very well, said the sea.
I have said my prayers.
I remember when dark gods
ruled a world like a thorn hedge
blazed with kerosene.
The wild evolution of human
want and waste, grown-up people
crowding like children in the rustle
of their mother's skirts.
Playing is a waste of time.
I broaden for sailboats, I pull
a cart. I discipline my spirit
in the harness room.

Some facts and conjecture about a terrible person

At her inauguration, the governor of Oklahoma swore, among other things, to offend the Constitution. You can't say she didn't warn us. That sound you hear is the odometer of history rolling back against its will. I would never go so far as to say Oklahoma is hell, but on days like today, with the smoke still hanging like a shadow over the ruins to the south & west, it's hard not to imagine a passing resemblance to Mordor: the oil derrick like a black gate in the valley of the capitol dome, the legislators slathering like orcs forging their iron caucuses and word-whet weaponry, and Mary Fallin towering above them, a flaming lidless eye stuttering across the scorched plain to search out and destroy anything beautiful and strange left in the world. I wonder if she even reads real books. I wonder if she realizes how that story ends.

Colonia

In the constellation of months,
August is the dullest star.
A world the color of ruin:
an aureole of napalm bleeding
into the atmosphere, stinging the raw
open throat of sky like a garrote
choking out strands of smoggy night,
scuds of storm flaring like a quick temper.

Sometimes it is our own god we are at war with.

So I wrap our longing in veils of linen,
pinned behind the ears.
One mouth pressed into the damp folds
searching out the other.

A street named for a bad man will never
be anything more or less than a stretch
of asphalt, with no capacity for good or evil,
no matter what you call it.
We give too much power to the naming
of things, as if the very act of naming
could somehow erase our scorched-earth pasts,
as if it could undo the harm that hungers
hot as a ticking bomb within our bellies.

Remember in the taxi how the driver
smelled of Damascus? Musky and animal,
hints of jasmine and cheese curd.
You could almost imagine the sand trapped
in the dark tangle glistening beneath his arms,
one flick of your tongue and the cab
would have showered in diamonds.

Sissy

Up the hill, up the hill. Snow falls heavy as a body. You clamber over and through it, a jar of teeth in one hand, a book you will never read in the other. Thinking that some people can sleep through anything.

Up the hill, up the hill. You remember his body in the cold morning light, quaking like a fault line stretching along the length of you. How the men working across the street pretended they weren't watching.

Up the hill, up the hill. This is the future you maybe didn't ask for. Another cold day, another unread book. You were learning how wars are fought. Quietly, mostly alone. Somewhere out of the way.

Up the hill, up the hill. This is what is left: the memory sprouting up, a familiar threat knocked toothless. A million bodies falling like snowflakes that will never melt on your tongue, all the names you can never say that will.

Quack

The duck goes quack
but sounds like a
dog barking
as it fans
one mottled wing
look how lovely
all the feathers
the feathers for
floating on air
the feathers for
floating on water
the same only one
is dry as bone
one is slavered
as dog's jaw
as swamp of
cunt open
for the man
the duck goes quack
but sounds like
a dog like a
man barking
if the man
fucks the man
the man
will fuck
the dog
the man
is gay (quack)
the dog is gay (quack)
the bone is
gay the shell blue sky
is gay (quack quack)
the feathers
fan the gay
like flame like
a wave a world
powder-downed

floating
in a sea of
gay the way
a cork floats
this changing
world frightens the
open water the
world doomed
as a duck as
doomed as a man
on the open sea.

Artificial Cloud

If the steel is left untreated the air will corrode
the planes before they ever reach the tower.

Moral: time eats what it cannot forget.

The last century was marrow,
now I live in a hollow bone.

Everyone needs a hobby.

I turn the bacon like an obsessive,
I can't keep my head out of the oven,
but nothing burns hot as Greenwood

on a Saturday night.

Inspiration is a nonrenewable resource.

In a busted boomtown everything runs on electric,
at night the transformers buzz like low flying planes.

Move on.
Move on.

Take down all the tall buildings so there is nothing left that scares us,
just a parking lot stretching north from midtown.

Leave no inscription to commemorate where the skyline crested,
just a memory we can skate across from Riverside

to where the buskers gathered on Brady,
where we danced to their music because sometimes
a body just needs to move.

The Bullet

When a bullet exits the chamber of a gun
the heat falls somewhere between
the temperature at which paper burns
and a horrific explosion, the kind that in movies
erupts like a volcanic blast in the background
just as the Good Guy whisks the girl to safety.

But there is nothing heroic about a dead boy.
Only the blood pluming beneath him in the rain,
the body like a broken bird.
A man stinking of sweat and fear.
The story unfolding a stiff plastic sheet,
what will and will not happen next.

Drift

Fear will eat your heart raw
like the buzzard picking at the jellied eye
of the possum carcass along the roadside.
It is growing late, but soon the streetlights
will flicker to life one by one, waking moons
to drown out the stars that can't help but look
like bullet holes riddling the darkening shift
of December sky from hem to hem.
The sow will slaughter the weakest suckling in her drift,
the spider will devour generations to survive the winter.
Ask the wild dog how it feels to know
the guns are always pointed at you.
Because they are, and knowing might save you.
Even guardian angels sometimes blink.

Going Native

Loosen your belt. Let's not pretend
austerity is a righteous condition.

If you shit like an animal,
you are probably an animal.

Yesterday the crows coiled like vertebrae
in the gangly spines of trees.

Bellwether!
Bellwether!

The God Builders

1.
Greatness begins in the raw materials.
The stones mumbled smooth
where the river runs quick and shallow
make the best constellations.
A virgin forest offered in immolation
smolders the finest kohl
for glyphing his name along the bathroom wall.
Be mindful of the consideration
you give the heart.
A muscle will atrophy and disintegrate
like a cobweb in the rain.
From the first beat it is already dying.

2.
The Man In The Box says Diligence,
and from window to window the blinds
part almost imperceptibly.
Paranoia travels invisible as sound,
parting negative space like a lifted wing.
In the belly of the silver bird we should all feel
holy and magnificent, but who can meditate
for the hum of machine imitating life?
White-knuckled hands grip the armrests:
we imagine it is our will that keeps us airborne.
We cannot hear the prayers
above the drone of the manmade heart.

3.
On a grey morning it is the
godhead of tightly bundled gold
adorning the breast of the meadowlark
the godhead of the music of the body
aged but waking again to usefulness
the godhead of the weight of you resting
upon my cheek then oh god

the head the pressure changes
the weather a microburst
the godpromise broken the flood
does not relent the flood
always threatens our godbodies
broken our trembling our supplication
our strong knees a godsend.

A Detour

This drought has lasted too long. The ditches are drinking their streetlamps, their guardrails. But the sun is ecstatic, it just keeps coming and coming, while the road pinned beneath it buckles and quakes until the traffic flows slow as neoprene. A boy watches in his rearview mirror from the car in front of me. He thinks I'm singing to him, and why shouldn't I be? Why not add some cinematic scope to this claustrophobic commute. I fear we suffer from a lack of song breaking-into, from a cancer of dancerless sidewalks and rooftops. Little boy, my baby-bird mouth could stretch wide enough to swallow the entirety of you: your still burning cigarette, your razor sharp sweep of too-cool hair, your Volkswagen, rims and all. I know a thing or two about dry spells, how thirst can smudge a pretty face with age like coal dust. How easy it is to miss your exit when singing to strangers on the expressway.

Oklahoma Is Burning

On Saturday the smoke began drifting over the city in black billows that rained ash like filthy snow. I stood on the lawn head back and mouth open until my tongue was dark and slick as shoe black. We hear stories about Pompeii and Herculaneum, the bodies found mummified in ash where they fell fleeing in the streets or huddled together in cupboards. No one remembers Stabiae or Oplontis, their faceless dead. Oklahoma is burning because I can't quit smoking. Oklahoma is burning because Sir Isaac Newton. Oklahoma is burning because Springfield 4, Drillers 2, because Perseid meteor shower. Oklahoma is burning because two boys kissing. Oklahoma is burning because we have our own fire to tend to. I feed it a hank of loose cat hair, an old shirt, a clipping from you left big toe.

Blunderbuss

When the war finally comes,
I wonder if I will wake in time to see it.
The low rumble of years has lulled me dormant.
If I were Robert Bly, I'd lead the charge
over the barricades with a dozen angry boys
half my age, spend the night in jail
and write letters to Tomas Transtromer
about finding Allen Ginsberg there, how we
passed the hours singing and chanting mantras
and reading poetry with the other malcontents.
But acceptance has made cowards of us all.
For every bitter boy wearing his heart like a bloody
baldric, another lines an empty promise with lead
and calls it a marriage bed. In the closeted
light of a bar it's hard to tell the difference between
want and need, between the conscientious objectors
and those who have come to die for the cause.
One mouth is so like another when your eyes are closed.
Perhaps it's the conflicts that spark between us
like the flicker of flint tonguing steel that
ultimately shape the histories we wanly share.
If tonight a man who is not my lover offers
me a drink, I will accept it as a reparation.
I'll let the liquor warm my belly like bravery.

I Hope You Don't Buy Into This

I arrange the room so that all roads
lead towards me or away, depending upon your perspective.

I come from a generation who have made a religion of casual despair,
which is to say even something incongruous as living can grow boring.

Layer into me like a feather: perhaps it's me who's gone
all goosey, a Pleiad, second star to the right

and straight on 'til morning!
I'm trying to come up with a reason to keep loving you.

Some small worship, a sacrifice in good faith couldn't hurt your case.
At the very least show me a sense of playfulness.

Bring unto me milk and honey, a bag of day old bread.
A fatted calf fresh from the country, someone no one will miss.

Read to me with gloves on, and just maybe I'll restore your
blighted crops—I am trying to recalibrate this tight coil of need

beyond the idea of the body as receptacle, as both temple and compost.
Look, see these hands?

The crooked spokes, the cratered half-moons?
They are everything I ever wanted.

I Drew You A Little Planet

My feet are balanced on your knee
more out of habit than necessity,
though my arches are killing me,
these shoes probably need replaced.
I know I shouldn't say I like you best
when you aren't speaking, but it's in
these quiet moments when you feel
most real, when the life I feel
in some small way is owed to me
seems closest. Notice how the sky
above us keeps on and on not falling?
Soon enough the moths, those fickle
philanderers, will leave our windows
for a brighter burning flame.

The Wolf on His Deathbed, Remorseless

Let it not be forgotten
that I was no more or less
than the sum of my instincts.

Would you blame me for hunger?
A girl moved like flame through the forest.
Even now she smolders the brush of these dead years.

Blood is untamable.
She was weak, I was not,
and this world will not let you choose.

Let Well Enough Alone

The sea said, Courage.
Let the faithless come
with their vices and cudgels,
their weaknesses and turbulent
futilities.
When the hour of need
arises, I shall not be found
among the shirkers.
Men stand and fall
by their convictions;
I yield to no man.

Stop-loss

Once inside the trailer, he cranks the oven to broil and props the door open against a rickety step stool. "Ghetto heater," he says, and I smile in a way I hope conveys collusion, because I know that his pretending I would understand what he means is its own kindness. We drink our beers in silence as the room gradually warms and our breath, fogging the air like bushelled rain, begins to dissipate. We are waiting to see what will happen next. Not in this moment, precisely, or even in this room. Just in general.

Lather. Rinse. Repeat.

In America
a woman owns her body
the same way gravity
rules the earth:
hypothetically, from beneath
the fat thumb of a man-made law.
To say that life
is a series of loss
followed by loss
is the worst kind of defeatism,
but sometimes the ugly thing
is the true thing.
The woman washes her hair
in a Japanese foot bath
because her womb
has become the kind of stone
that fixes you
to one place,
because gravity
pushes rather than pulls.
Only with a head
of clean and shining hair
can the Kingdom of Heaven
be hers.

Dear Lord

My lover holds court
like a duke on the street corner.
He is a kind and generous lord,
he seeks to share what he has learned
with his people.
My lover is wise, he uses words
like Hegemony and Obsequence
with a regal nod of his head,
the flourish of his arm as fine
as a banner snapping in the breeze.
He tells me to love is to know
violence, to move inside someone
is to know another kind of murder:
the deep stab like pressing a tack
through the wall of a rubber band.
The taut resistance,
the sudden pop and slow give.

As the Crow Flies

Carl, as we drove through the Ozarks
I watched the mist ghosting down the ridge and wondered
if I would live long enough to see all those trees
taken down, and I am afraid the answer is yes.

We were only a few miles from where the police
killed that boy, and it struck me like a strap across the back
that I might have to explain which one, how some small
menace could crack the façade of our guilty city
and history recycle itself filthy as poisoned ground water.

I'm not sure what it means that we never have these conversations,
the messy discussions where one misplaced opinion
can change the way you see a person sure
as the sharp end of a paring knife,

but I know that while we are born to a litany of possible dooms,
the sun still rises and sets and in between stretch
long days we must try to live through and consider what has been
given us and what is left for us to choose.

Carl, I want to know why some men are born
with a need to fill or empty all the spaces,
but never the capacity to leave things as they found them.

Carl, I want to know why all this fucking and still
no baby, just softened middles and thinning hair,
the bodies of two men pressing up against oblivion.

The Postulant

Unleavened

At night I dream of monsters,
scales that slide like glaciers over glass.
The dead speak to me in whispers
blunted as a bird's clipped wing.

The morning is a bowl of clean milk.
The day is a loaf of kibbled bread,
coarse and many-grained,
rough with nourishment.

The sky is falling

They knocked down another house in the neighborhood. One loud naked morning two more will go up in its place. They call Venice the City of Falling Angels because the people who live there resist change with the sad veracity of a body battling back against decrepitude. The buildings crumble and molder like an aging face, the city rife with the terrible beauty of life turning in on itself. We will call this the Summer of Falling Bricks, but later it won't be the empty lots, barren as defunded excavations, that you remember, nor the biblical implications of another hurricane in the gulf while Oklahoma blistered with drought, drawing the crickets like locusts in swarms. But the image of a single cricket behind the toilet, not dead but dying, how it seemed for a moment to shudder and grow in the nourishment of your gaze, will startle you awake intermittently for years. You want so badly for everything to be beautiful.

There—no, there

When he says put it back, I want you
to think about the places that have gone without.
Yes, I know how that sounds.
There's something wrong with things
not touching, with all these empty spaces.
My mother was always this way.
Haven't I told you the story?
The beginning and ending are always the same,
the middle depends upon the audience.
If the cat moves in with the people
down the street, it isn't that they stole him.
A living thing can never really belong
to another living thing.

Ordinary Monsters

Once when I was a child
walking alone to my grandma's house
I saw something scary in the woods.
I still remember the snap of the twig
like a crunching of bone
that startled me silent mid-song,
the dun-colored fur covering the leg
that stepped out from behind the trunk
of an old pecan tree,
foreign and sapling-thick.
How I ran, clumsily and blindly, fearing
the thing all children secretly fear most:
the fairytale come to life.

We grow up and the world grows
smaller. The monsters it breeds
have become a more ordinary variety,
hairy-legged and hungry,
some wearing the faces of people
I tell myself I might want to love.
But even as I feel myself opening
to receive them, I shut my eyes tight
as two fists, I can't bear to look back
at the forest behind me.

Horse

Mother said they found him
already gone, where he had
lain in the sun to warm himself
on a dry patch of grass
near the barn,
as horses love to do.
It couldn't be called surprising
that the horse should have passed
this way or, indeed, at all,
having lived through twenty-eight
winters, mostly blind
for the last half dozen or so
and far past the age for riding,
back swayed as an old
bridge that no one trusts
enough to cross any longer.
But it's part of
what elevates us above
a clumsy gallop of meat and bone,
this insistence on defining
ourselves by the things
we have had or had happen,
the resistance to the falling
away of the familiar
as time canters forward.
Even while realizing
as I try to do
that something as yet unseen
is already preparing to fill
the vacant space,
that there is still happy
to be had, wide and green
as this open field
that will seem
a little emptier
come spring.

Hobby Horse

My lover fashions wind chimes
from the bones of small animals
and hangs them all over the house.
At night the wind moves through them,
filling the rooms
with the tiny songs of the dead
and he cannot help but dance,
contorting his body to a rhythm
only he can decipher.
As a child this was a game he would play
to frighten his parents,
flinging his arms and legs akimbo
like a rag doll coming to life in fits and starts.
He was a difficult child, always
drawing on walls, always hiding food everywhere.
Even now he pulls a bowl
of fruit from the dresser drawer.
He splits a peach with a small silver knife,
names one half Nick and the other Norah.
Look, he says, holding them out to me.
Finally: children.

We Are the Breakers of Our Own Hearts

I rise
and there is no metaphor in it,
just the song of the body
plucked on tired strings.
I used to call the night
my unkempt familiar:
my throat was thick with wet leaves,
I had a cunt like a storm drain.
But the morning is a stranger beast,
all fang and feral fur.
Canopic jars full of light stacked
against the basement wall
and your fingerprints, god bless you,
on every single one.

Red River Redux

Traveling south on the turnpike I feel I am seeping down to the tips of my muddy roots. The past pulls like the sea, as deep and as selfish. An open trench of hunger roiling at the bottom. I pass a sign for a new casino and consider stopping, but I'm not in the Choctaw Nation and the Kickapoo have enough already. The highway is lined with hanging trees, fields and streams so red you would swear the soil dreams in blood. At the end of the road a small dog who is just as red is waiting. Her bowl is probably empty. She probably needs to pee.

A long walk down a narrow hallway

I wrap the gifts in brightly colored paper as thin as old skin, as celebratory. What began in darkness. Then tiny pinpricks of light, before the whole of the world broke over you like yolk as it rent a small part of itself to accept you. Would you have saved the old teeth as they fell, or planted them in the ground to see what might grow? The wisp of cord like a knot of cured meat. Sustenance for a long journey. Tonight we celebrate this rough ride slick as a body. That which I can take into my mouth. That which burns like light falling upon new skin.

Winter in the Spite House

So many things I thought finished
left undone like an errant shoelace.
A cake half-baked,
another year on this dimpled rock.

I would rather be regretted
than remembered fondly.
Better to rip through your gut like dysentery
than wash your feet in this rusty bucket.

Passover

The street tonight is a chaos of swirling leaves.
As though they've fallen all at once,
as if the trees could suddenly no longer
bear the golden weight of them,
their endless insistence on synthesis.
I sense a menace in the air, feral as November,
building like the steam that rolls from the grate.
The pink ambulance won't save you any faster.
On the inside we are pink as wet taffy,
capable of such elegant tragedies.
I would murder a hundred babies in their beds
and seal our door in bloody pitch to guarantee
safe passage through this hungry harm.
As helpless as we are, as wombless.

Dream

From the moment the car lurches from the road
and begins to tumble, improbably,
end over end
gravity feels as hollow
as any promise made in summer

but, oh! how soothing the warmth
of the water
when it envelops you like the rain
in the place you grew up

He Wants To Be Alex Dimitrov

He wants to be Alex Dimitrov,
but he's too old for the sleeping around.
He can't manage the perfectly-manicured
scruff, the black leather and cigarettes.
He never thought he'd live this long
in a world so sharp with dangers.
Thirsty as sharks' teeth, row upon row
salivating to burst to the bloody fore.
He doesn't believe cancer exists
in predestined dirty bombs built into the
razor wire ramps of the double helix,
which ought to be comforting.
But not when you believe, as he does,
that all cancers hide like cowards
deep within cells wearing the bodies of
people you love. Sometimes on their
lips or in their blood, lurking in the bed
scheming their way across the hip
of one unwittingly dying body
to the next. He wouldn't be surprised if,
at the root of it, was just another reason to hate
the goddamn rhesus monkey.

If I Could Reach That Far

I would take your hand
and tell you
squeeze once for yes, twice for no.

I would say,   look
there will always be witnesses
to an unraveling:

fence post

stray dog

sun like a hollowed out god.

Moss always grows thickest
on the north side of the tree.

Wrap your arms around the trunk
        of an oak.
Rough and grey as elephant skin,
pulsing with memory.

Threading the Needle
for Debra

From the heart of my city
at night the sphere of this fat
earth seems almost endless,
but the air still feels close
enough to take its liberties,
moving over and under
my clothes to hold me
the way it held your breasts
against your narrow chest,
bare and honest as joy,
while you straddled the
passenger seat, dark squall
of hair troubling behind you
like a storm cloud,
that last barbarian summer
when your hunger
was still your own.

In the breeze the trees
assume Vedic poses:
Sucirandhrasana,
threading the needle.
Ujjayi pranayama,
the conqueror breath.
Somewhere nearby laughter
falls like pennies on
the empty street,
lovely and deceptive
as a fine sky on a cold night.
A woman, maybe a little
drunk, very much alive.

Derecho

Tonight I'm feeling sad.
Nothing dramatic, just a feeling
like a lyric half-forgotten,
the hollow timbre of a phantom limb.

Across the street they haul away
the fallen tree in buckskinned segments.
The neighbor's porch light will stay on
all night: she knows it was a close call.

Root Cellar

The rain always comes too late to make any difference. I'm tired of negotiating with the dead. The sour stench of scorched tomato vines, the ruined fruit of the people we used to be. The season has come for storing the pasts we have grown in a cool dry place until we learn to make use of them. For the gentle nodding of heads, the soft clucking of tongues at the lateness of the hour.

Multitude

1.

The first time I died
the moon hung heavy & low-slung,
the light where it broke
through the tree line
spelling out calamity
in a language old as cave-speak.
I moved through the ragged dark
lithe as any caged thing
that's happened upon a lock left unlatched,
the distant call and response
of the men and their hounds
closing in around me
sure as any noose.
The body don't know the difference
between frolic and flight,
just keeps forcing
one foot in front of the other.
And I'll tell you something else:
when that coarse loop does slip
closed, you hear the sound
of the snap quicker than the body
knows what to do with it.

2.

The second time I died
I was an old, old woman.
I wore a chain around my neck
that held a lock of hair from a sister
who had died long before me.
One by one the faces gathered,
so many pale moons orbiting my beside
it seemed every summer night
I had selfishly dwindled
drifted in through the open window.
It was hard to tell the faces of the living
from the faces of the dead.

I thought how everything comes in threes,
how we honor the dead
by fearing for them.

Somewhere in the house mirrors were covered
with my second-best sheets.
Somewhere the scent of lavender, the scent
of candle wax: the scent of waiting.
It had been a good life.

I had owned many beautiful things,
there had been time to read.
Most of the children had loved me.
My husband had taken only
what he needed of me and nothing more,
and if, like a rutting buck, he had ever
wandered in search of warmer thickets,
he'd had the decency
to keep me ignorant.

The lilacs bloomed. The whippoorwill
called, and the mockingbird
called back.

Even with all this,
it is never enough.

3.
For my third death, I will need you to close your eyes.
Imagine the highest bridge in a city of tall bridges.
You are the man standing on the wrong side of the railing,
your back to an iron girder in relief against the setting sun
so that you are little more than shadow to any passing cars.

Below you a river runs like a red ribbon,
and every stone you drop punches a hole in the current
deep and dark as the holes you had always felt you were born with,
holes you tried to fill with a mortar of wife and children,
late nights at work and a steady stream of coffee and booze.

When you fall you wonder if you will become the kind of story
bored teenagers will use to scare a little life into their Saturday nights.
If you will be reduced to a shadow on the bridge,
a cry muffled in the dark
the sound of weeping echoing on the wind, for what you gladly forfeit
the young will only read as a tragedy.

You wonder how much of it will be true.

When you fall, you see yourself as if from a distant bank,
the ink of your descending form sliding down the sky an Icarus,
perfectly and beautifully broken, like the pelicans in Galveston,
wheeling into the water over and over until they're ruined by it,
until they're blinded by the joy of it.

4.
This time I willed myself into being.

The way some are born with the memory of the womb
still enveloping them soft as gloved leather,
I came to the world with the knowledge of the before
tucked in my brain, flashless photographs
from the bottom of a mineshaft.

The way the darkness at times undulated like water
in the bottom of a shallow bowl.
How consciousness dawned, gradual as skin
knits itself along the frame of the body,
seamless and without incidence.

The Otherworld was a blanket whose nap
had worn thin and threadbare, membranous.
And through this film many sounds passed
I would have called music, had I the capacity to name them.
A cacophony of seagulls and car horns

Metal scraping across the vocal folds of falling buildings,
the percussion of blood rushing in and out of bodies,
bodies torn to pieces, bodies pressing into other bodies
over and over, looking for a way back in.

I listened and the sound was a current and I
was the stone that parted it.
I listened and the sound was the sea and I
was the conch that tried and failed to hold it,
the ear pressed against the pearled rim
to hear a memory of the roar, more wish than water.

I learned how worlds are built and destroyed,
usually at the same time.
The woman who discovers a lump,
small and hard as fear, beneath her left breast.
The little girl smashing ladybugs in a garden
who notices for the first time
that even the smallest things have shadows
when the light is right.

But then I found myself alone
in a cave where everything shimmered with damp,
cavernous as the belly of a whale.

Where I had come to a body, the fingers and toes.
A sky splitting suddenly above me.
The hot rush of blood, the burn of light on my dolphin skin.
I never saw what was waiting on the other side,

but I wonder in that moment, just before the Light was snuffed back out,
if they were more afraid of or for
my ancient glittering eyes.

5.
The last time I died
I had been born with holes
again, only this time
I had filled the holes with god
and god was hungry.

The voice of god is the dull
ache of an impacted tooth
throbbing just below the surface of your gum
It is the phantom

pain that lingers long after the tooth
is torn away, and nothing remains
but a ragged copper canyon.

It is selfish and irrevocable
as gravity,
patient as the sea.
It will whisper to you
the ways of violence,
how to use your body like a weapon.
The balled fist, the hard cock,
all the tools to drive love like a dog
from beneath your feet.

It knows your fears
and will show them to you
through a broken mirror:
in a world that is always healing,
you will see only hurt.

And you,
you become the mouth of god.
You will want to hurt it back.

6.
I dreamed I saw my life through a yellow veil.
Old lace the color of nicotine.
I sat on the porch and watched you
wander through the ashcan of our lawn,
picking your way between gravestones
scattered here and there like cigarette butts,
searching out my name.
It seemed for a moment that all of them were mine.
I felt the earth grow weary with the burden
of brunting the enormity of me.
The moon was full as a tick, bright
as a blossoming poppy. I lit a cigarette
and waited for it to give up its dusty ghost,
for you to look up and recognize me
as someone you knew or would want to know.

Beneath the Dead Elm

Just below the lip of the raised bed
a green tongue of iris pushes its way up
through the soft palate of earth.
You tell me this happens every year,
the difference between annuals and perennials,
and I think how we begin each day with mouths
full of futures we shed by the hour like deciduous teeth.
The mockingbird knows the secret to survival
is pretending: not in happiness, which is very real,
but that we knew all along where to find it.

Four Walls

Look, this is how it happens:
In a room.
Four walls and a floor.
High ceiling, windows
that allow too much light
in the morning.
A room is a room is
(usually) a room,
but this is the room
where you first learned to love
the light and take it in
like music.
This is the room
you first opened to him
with the tremor of a promise
that yearns to be broken.
If this room were a river
it would move swift and dangerous,
twisting over stones like
a knotted snake.
If this room were a fall,
it would be a long one
you would fight all the way down,
refusing to embrace the inevitable
even as the earth reached up
to snatch you.

The Visitor

Age came to me like a golem in the night,
tracking the muck of years across the brick floor
and bare white walls that lead to my bedroom.
He said, for everything I have stolen from you,
I have given you a gift.
The knowledge you carry like a sack
over your shoulder will give you weight
when the winds are changing.
The lines I embed in the bark
of your body are a compass
to center yourself when the spin of the world
unsteadies your balance.
His voice was an echo of the wind
in my father's throat,
but I refused to recognize him.
I told him: I do not know your face.
He said, my tongue is a shem that bears your name.
Beneath this clay, mined from the narrow banks
of your beginnings, are your mother's cheekbones
and your grandfather's high, fine forehead.
Then throw open my closets, I cried, and tell me—
how do I clean the ruined gown
of this life I have lived?
There are no mysteries left in the world, he said.
A boy in a dress is just a boy in a dress.
Don't read so much into it.

Notes

"Partly in earnest, partly in jest," "Handsome Young Man," "Let Well Enough Alone," "Seeing, keenly centered," and "The Steam Cars on Monday" are all found poems taken from the text of The Late George Apley by John P. Marquand. They were written as part of The Found Poetry Review 2013 National Poetry Month initiative, The Pulitzer Remix Project.

"Movie Bachelors At Home, 1935" is inspired by a photograph of Cary Grant and Randall Scott from a trade feature with the same title, circa 1935.

"Troublesome Creek" is inspired by several accounts of the "Blue Fugates" of Troublesome Creek, Kentucky, who suffered from a rare genetic disorder known as argyria, which resulted in the skin taking on a blue pigment.

"Hobby Horse" was selected by Emotive Fruition, an NYC-based poetry performance series, for their 2016 Pride Poetry Show, sponsored by Lambda Literary. For this performance, the piece was performed by Obie Award- winner Michael Potts.

Many of these poems appeared, sometimes in different versions, in the chapbook Going Native, released by Red Bird Chapbooks in 2014.